Daily Life
in a
Covered Wagon

Paul Erickson

PUFFIN BOOKS

PUFFIN BOOKS
Published by the Penguin Group
Penguin Books USA Inc., 375 Hudson Street, New York, New York 10014, U.S.A.
Penguin Books Ltd, 27 Wrights Lane, London W8 5TZ, England
Penguin Books Australia Ltd, Ringwood, Victoria, Australia
Penguin Books Canada Ltd, 10 Alcorn Avenue, Toronto, Ontario, Canada M4V 3B2
Penguin Books (N.Z.) Ltd, 182-190 Wairau Road, Auckland 10, New Zealand

Penguin Books Ltd, Registered Offices: Harmondsworth, Middlesex, England

First published in Great Britain by Hamlyn Children's Books, an imprint of Reed Children's Books Limited, 1994
First published in the United States of America by the Preservation Press, 1994
Published in Puffin Books, 1997

1 3 5 7 9 10 8 6 4 2

Library of Congress Catalog Card Number 96-70377

Puffin Books ISBN 0-14-056212-5

Printed in Hong Kong

CONTENTS

Going West

I n the 1840s the United States doubled in size (*see map right*). By either negotiation, war, or purchase, it acquired most of Oregon, Texas, California and the American Southwest. There was a great desire to expand into these new and little known territories, and several

Right: *Western Expansion of the United States by 1853.*

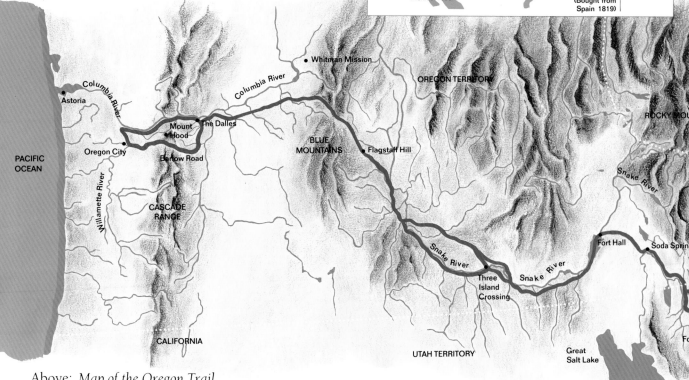

Above: *Map of the Oregon Trail*

people went out to explore the region and came back with reports of rich soil and good opportunities for farmers. Interest in the west grew, until it was said that "if hell were in the west, Americans would cross heaven to get there." Newspaper editors spoke of the "Manifest Destiny" to make the United States stretch "from sea to shining sea." "Oregon Fever" was just one part of this western expansion. According to the "boosters" who encouraged people to move west, Oregon was a paradise "flowing with milk and honey." It was even said that pigs ran around ready cooked with knives and forks sticking in them so that anyone could have a slice.

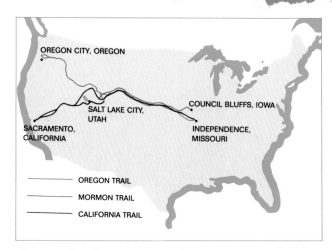

Above: *The Three Main Trails West*

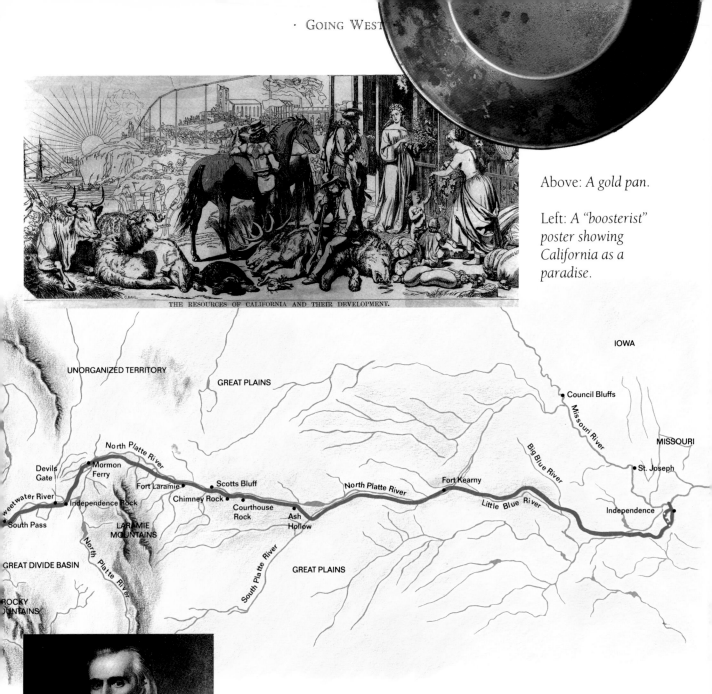

Above: *A gold pan.*

Left: *A "boosterist" poster showing California as a paradise.*

THE RESOURCES OF CALIFORNIA AND THEIR DEVELOPMENT.

Above: *James K. Polk became President in 1844 because he promised Americans "All of Oregon or War!" In the early 1840s, part of Oregon still belonged to Great Britain.*

The journey west was very dangerous, and even Horace Greeley, the newspaper editor famous for saying "Go west, young man!" warned against making it. However, the success of the first wagon train in 1843 proved him wrong, and soon thousands were emigrating to Oregon. Despite the difficulties of crossing "the Great American desert," there were several reasons to go west. Some people, like the Mormons, wanted to be free to practice their religion; others, like the "Forty-Niners" of the 1849 California gold rush, hoped to find gold and get rich; and others wanted to make better lives for themselves farming on the fertile land.

Most of the pioneers wanted to bring "civilization" with them: Fashions and entertainments as well as laws, schools, and colleges. They wanted to stay in touch with what was happening back east, no matter how different their new lives were.

THE FAMILY

T he year is 1853, and the Larkin family are on their way to Oregon. For a journey of over 2,000 miles, lasting nearly five months, a covered wagon will be their home. Like so many other Americans, they have made the momentous decision to "emigrate," that is, to leave the settled states east of the Mississippi for a new and better life in the West.

HIRAM LARKIN

HETTY LARKIN

Above and right: *Books like Palmer's* Journal of Travels over the Rocky Mountains *and* Horn's Overland Guide *are Mr. Larkin's favorite reading matter.*

Mr. Larkin has considered very carefully before deciding to take the trip. On his 110-acre farm in Indiana, he is able to provide the basic necessities of life for his family. He is certainly better off than a laborer, who might earn only $100 a year, but he finds it hard to make a profit, and he is worried that the soil in Indiana is "worn out."

Hiram Larkin, age 35, is of Scots-Irish ancestry. Like his father and grandfather before him, he is a hard-working farmer. He did not get swept up in the first bout of "Oregon Fever" in the mid-1840s, but his views changed when he began to read reports of the trip and the richness of the Oregon soil. Now he has sold his farm and stock in Indiana and taken his family by steamboat to the "jumping-off point" of Independence, Missouri, where the overlanders meet up and make preparations before starting on their long overland trek.

Hetty Gilkey married Hiram Larkin when she was 18 years old. Now she is 33. Like Hiram, she comes from a farming family. Hetty did not want to leave Indiana at first, but she changed her mind after the Donation Land Act was passed in 1850. This law cut the amount of land an Oregon settler could claim from 640 acres to 320 acres, but allowed him to claim 320 acres for his wife. Hetty liked the idea of owning land. She helped to save money for the trip, which could cost over $1,200. They sold their land for $5 an acre, but were still short, so Hetty borrowed $400 from her brother.

THE CHILDREN

Rachel (14), Abraham (10), Rebecca (7), and Margaret (3)

At the time of their emigration to Oregon, Hiram and Hetty Larkin have four children – fewer than most farming families of that time. A fifth child (born between Rachel and Abraham) died of scarlet fever when he was two years old.

The eldest surviving child is Rachel, now nearly 15. Since having scarlet fever as a little girl, Rachel has been "sickly," and her mother worries that the trip to Oregon will be too much for her heart.

Her father, however, points out that the trip west has restored many sick people to good health.

Abraham, or Abe, and Rebecca are both thrilled to be traveling to Oregon and cannot wait to get started.

Little Margaret, who has just turned three, is too young to understand quite what is happening. She clings to her mother's skirts and seems completely bewildered by all the changes going on around her.

MATTHEW BELKNAP

Matthew, or Matt, Belknap is an 18-year-old orphan from St. Louis. After his parents died in a cholera epidemic, Matt lived with an uncle, but ran away to Independence because he was badly treated. Now Matt has been hired by Hiram Larkin. In return for "a man's work," which will be mainly hunting and looking after cattle, Matt will join the Larkin household for the trip to Oregon.

THE WAGON

A ll Mr. Larkin's guidebooks say that the key to a successful journey to Oregon is a good wagon. It must be strong, in order to carry a load of perhaps 2,000 lbs. over rough and mountainous country, and light, in order not to strain the oxen pulling it. Rather than risk using the family's rickety old farm wagon, Mr. Larkin decided to buy a new wagon in Independence.

"The wagon looks so nice, with its white cover. It is plenty high enough for me to stand straight under the roof. Once it starts rolling, with everything packed away ship-shape, it will be a prairie schooner indeed!" Mrs. Larkin's Diary

Above: *Wagon trains waiting to begin the journey.*

At $110, it is the most expensive thing he has bought for the trip. Even Mrs. Larkin is pleased with it. She has decided to call it "Hoosier Home." This is because the Larkins came from Indiana, and people from that state are sometimes called "hoosiers."

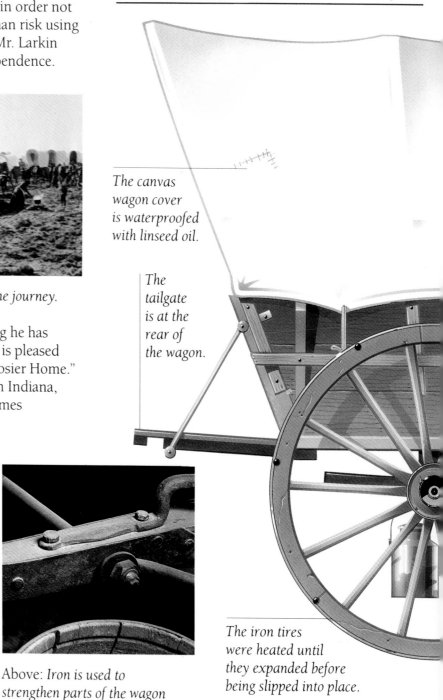

The canvas wagon cover is waterproofed with linseed oil.

The tailgate is at the rear of the wagon.

The iron tires were heated until they expanded before being slipped into place.

Above: *The cover is threaded through with a "puckering string" at each end, so that it can be opened and closed.*

Above: *Iron is used to strengthen parts of the wagon such as the axles and wheels.*

Left: *The wagons were parked in a circle at night to give protection from wolves, cattle thieves, and the wind.*

Below: *The body of the wagon is a box four feet wide by ten feet long. The Larkins' wagon is of the "Murphy" type with slightly flaring sides.*

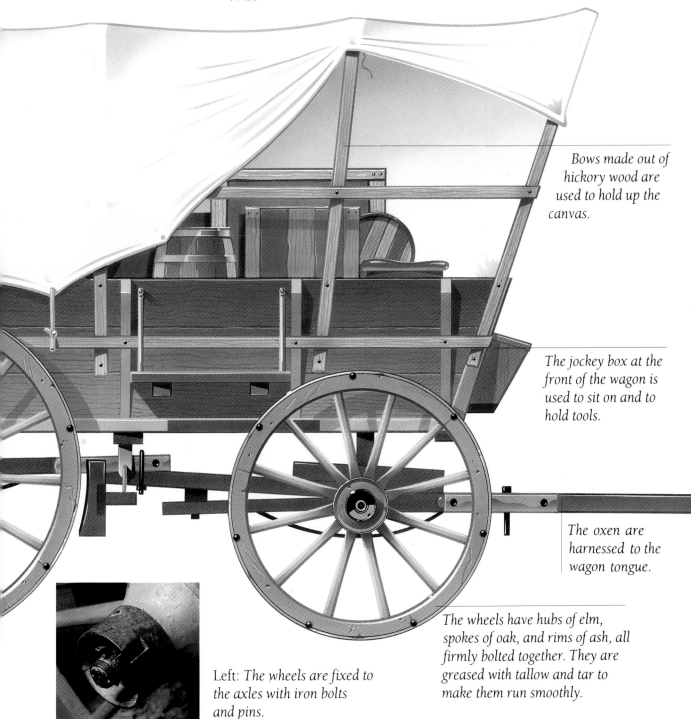

Bows made out of hickory wood are used to hold up the canvas.

The jockey box at the front of the wagon is used to sit on and to hold tools.

The oxen are harnessed to the wagon tongue.

Left: *The wheels are fixed to the axles with iron bolts and pins.*

The wheels have hubs of elm, spokes of oak, and rims of ash, all firmly bolted together. They are greased with tallow and tar to make them run smoothly.

INSIDE THE WAGON

The Larkins' wagon is not a traveling house like a modern caravan, it is more of a storage space. It is loaded with provisions for the long journey and for fitting out a new farmstead in Oregon. The tools that Mr. Larkin will need for farming are strapped to the sides, and spare parts for the wagon are slung

Above: Barrels, rope, iron pots, tin plates, ladles, nails, a chair, and a rifle will all be needed in Oregon, as well as on the wagon train.

underneath. Inside, there is a leather trunk filled with medicines, a bottle of matches tightly corked to keep out moisture, the big family bible, and other special treasures carried from Indiana. One wooden box contains the pots, pans, and cutlery that the Larkins will need for the trip. Another box, carefully stowed away, is filled with bolts of cloth, good linen, and the family's "best clothes," which will not be taken out again until the Larkins arrive in Oregon. Yet another box contains plant cuttings, since Mr. Larkin hopes to have an orchard on his new farm. Mrs. Larkin watches as the men load the wagon to make sure that the more precious things are tucked out of harm's way.

Above: A large trunk stowed in the bottom of the wagon keeps family treasures and good clothes safe during the journey.

Above: A scythe and hoe are tied to the side of the wagon. A tin pitcher holds grease for the axles.

10

Blankets, pillows, and featherbeds are wrapped up in canvas ground cloths. Tents, poles, rope, and stakes are stacked to one side, propped in place by a few pieces of furniture.

The Larkins' everyday clothing hangs from hooks fixed to the hickory bows, while pockets in the canvas walls hold cord, small arms, and Mrs. Larkin's sewing things and toiletries. Overhead a lantern is suspended, along with a ready shotgun.

Above: *Hardtack or "pilot bread" could be kept for long periods of time. This dates from the 1860s!*

Food for the Journey

Stout double canvas sacks, their seams well stitched by Mrs. Larkin back in Indiana, are now filled up with the huge amounts of food recommended in the guidebooks – 100 lbs of flour for each adult, 70 lbs of bacon, 30 lbs of "pilot bread" or hardtack, beans, rice, coffee, sugar, dried fruits, baking soda, vinegar – all bought from the stores in Independence.

Above: *A calico blouse, a cotton apron, and other finery will remain packed until arrival in Oregon.*

Below: *Eggs, china, and other fragile items are packed in barrels of cornmeal.*

Communications

Mrs. Larkin packs her pen away carefully. Like many overlanders, she will keep a diary and write letters to relatives back East, which can be left for posting at various places along the way. For other messages, there is a "roadside telegraph" or "bone express": Messages are left for following wagon trains, posted on a cleft stick or scribbled on sun-bleached bones. Sometimes they gave good advice, such as "For God's sake do not taste this water. It is poisonous," but some pranksters left misleading messages to confuse other travelers.

Left: *Once the fire is lit, Mrs. Larkin roasts the coffee beans over it before grinding them. Then she puts the pot on the fire to boil.*

Right: *An overlander's breakfast included johnnycake, bacon, and coffee.*

DAYBREAK

A t 4 a.m. the night watch fire their guns to let everyone know that it is daybreak. Quickly, the overlanders pull on their boots or shoes, throw a few garments over the clothes they have slept in, and set about their morning tasks.

Mrs. Larkin cooks the breakfast. First, she has to make a fire. A steady wind is always blowing across the prairies, so she must dig a shallow trench. Then she must find some fuel. On the high plains a wagon train might travel for days without seeing a single tree, but the pioneers soon discovered that dried buffalo droppings, or "buffalo chips," made a clean, hot fire, with little smoke or smell. In the mountains, dead sage brush would do instead.

Even with her trench filled with fuel, Mrs. Larkin often has difficulty lighting the fire. Sometimes she resorts to sprinkling the fuel with gunpowder.

Above: *A mill for grinding coffee beans.*

12

Breakfast

Pancakes are breakfast favorites as they require only flour, water, baking soda, and a skillet to cook them in, but Mrs. Larkin often bakes bread in a dutch oven, using risen dough that she prepares the evening before. On other days she makes soda biscuits, muffins, or cornmeal johnnycakes. Beans, well greased with slab bacon and slowly simmered through the night in the ashes of the fire, are a popular breakfast dish, as is fried meat, which is served with a gravy made of pan drippings and flour. The overlanders like to begin the day with a hearty meal.

Coffee is the all-purpose trail thirst-quencher, served at every meal. The overlanders rarely drink plain water, since it is usually muddy or polluted, and tastes so disgusting that sometimes even the animals refuse it. Only disguised by the strong flavor of coffee does it become palatable to man – and beast.

Above: *Cast-iron skillets and a long-handled pan for making popcorn.*

"There is a great scarcity of wood, and we are compelled to cook our food with buffalo chips. This has caused many of the ladies to act very cross, but necessity is a great leveler, and now we all must search for them." Mrs. Larkin's Diary

Above and below: *Carefully designed portable "canteens" like these could carry plates, bowls, cutlery, jars for sugar and salt, and larger items such as flasks for vinegar.*

HITCHING UP THE WAGON

While Mrs. Larkin is preparing breakfast, the men of the party round up the livestock. The riding horses are close at hand. They have been hobbled to the wagons during the night in case they are stolen by Indians. The cattle, however, have been left free to graze where they like, and by dawn some have wandered far from the camp in search of the tastiest grass.

Overlanders traveled in different ways. Farming families like the Larkins usually chose oxen to pull the wagon the 2,000 mile journey, since these animals are very strong. However, men bound for the California gold fields often chose a pack-train of mules that could go faster than a covered wagon, even when carrying panniers (*see below*) filled with heavy supplies.

Left: *Overlanders bound for the gold fields would carry their supplies in a pair of panniers strapped over a mule's back.*

Right: *On hard or rocky trails iron shoes protected the oxen's feet.*

After the cattle have been driven into the corral of circled wagons and sorted out, Mr. Larkin yokes up his team of six oxen. While many overlanders used oxen from their old farmsteads, Mr. Larkin purchased these in Independence. He wanted them fresh for the journey, and he also knew from his reading in the guidebooks that oxen in Missouri were cheap and accustomed to eating the tough grasses of the prairie. Some overlanders did use mules, which were tough, relatively speedy, and could survive on cottonwood bark, but the vast majority preferred oxen. Although oxen were slower than mules, they fared much better in muddy conditions and could survive on little food. Most of the overlanders used oxen on their farms back east and were experienced at handling them. Besides that, oxen were relatively cheap. They cost only $55 to $65 per yoke (2 oxen), while mules might be as much as $110 each. Like the Larkins, most overlanders have one or two saddle horses. However, horses were not used to pull the wagons until the later years on the trail because they could not work well with such poor feed.

In addition to their oxen, the Larkins have two milk cows. Rachel and Abraham have the task of milking them every morning and evening. In the evening the Larkin family drink the milk fresh with their supper, but in the morning Mrs. Larkin puts the milk into a churn, which she hangs from the back of the wagon. On the trail she does not have time to make butter the way she did back in Indiana, but without it even her tasty biscuits and pancakes are too dry to eat. Fortunately, she has learned a shortcut. As the wagon bumps along, the milk is shaken so vigorously that large balls of butter will form with no hand churning at all.

Above:
Wooden ox yoke.

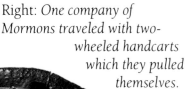

Right: *One company of
Mormons traveled with two-
wheeled handcarts
which they pulled
themselves.*

Right: *Otto Sommer's painting of the Oregon trail,* Westward Ho!

Above: *With this folding pocket sundial and compass, the Captain can tell both time and direction.*

ROLLING THE TRAIN

At 7 a.m. a bugle sounds. As the women bundle away the last of the cookware, the men shout commands to their teams. "Roll the wagons!" shouts the captain of the wagon train. The first wagon moves out of the camp, and soon the whole company has spread out across the prairie in a growing cloud of dust.

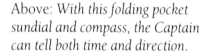

Above: *The pepperbox pistol was named after its black gunpowder.*

There are 60 families in the Larkins' wagon train. Some of these are old friends from Franklin County, Indiana, with whom the Larkins have been sharing travel plans for many months, and there is a larger party from Illinois. Finally, there are assorted smaller groups from Missouri.

Even after the trail has become well worn, few overlanders set off alone, preferring the support and security of a large group. Together, they make up a sort of village on wheels, with men of all trades amongst the travelers. Like a village, the wagon train needed some sort of government, and meetings were held to elect a captain.

One early party even worked out a miniature government system that included laws and courts. When the people chosen to administer it refused to do chores like guard duty, the ordinary "citizens" grew fed up and put a stop to it.

Above: *In a wagon train, just as in the army, a bugle announced the major moments of the day.*

"**We have elected Captain Bonner, of Weston, Missouri, to lead our company. The Illinois men might have preferred one of their own, but even they must admit that he is an expert with a bullwhip and handles the cattle very well.**"
Mr. Larkin's Diary

Below: *The captain's spyglass, pipe, and a fold-away knife for carving and whittling.*

The Captain

James J. Bonner is captain of the Larkins' wagon train. A man of great experience, he already has crossed the plains in both directions and knows the trail quite well, so the Larkins' party decided to hire him instead of a professional guide. Captain Bonner is responsible for all the major decisions about the wagon train: The route they will travel, the time for starting and halting each day, the site where they will camp for the night, the site for the midday "nooning" (*see page 29*), the posting of guards and the daily rotation of the wagons. Rotation was necessary because no one wanted to be at the end of a dusty wagon train every day!

Captain Bonner is worried because there has been a lot of rain. Although this means that there will be a good supply of grass for the animals, swollen streams and mud will slow down the wagons. The party will need to make good time to get to the mountain passes before they are blocked by snow. If they fail, they will have to spend the winter on the eastern side of the Blue Mountains.

ON THE TRAIL

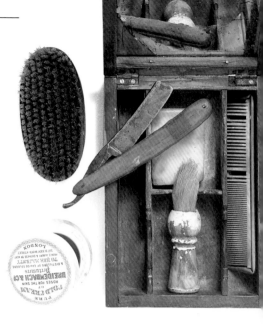

W ith no springs or cushioned seats, the Larkins' wagon was far too uncomfortable to ride in. Most of the pioneers traveled the 2,000 miles of the Oregon trail on foot. If it rained, they simply put on oilskin ponchos or unfurled umbrellas and marched on. They did not have to walk fast, however, since the wagons lumbered along at the rate of only one or two miles per hour. Children who got tired might hitch a short ride on the wagon tongue. Sick people who had to ride in the wagon were put on featherbeds and padded round with pillows to relieve the worst of the jolting.

Mr. Larkin walks alongside his oxen, shouting commands like "gee" ("go right") and "haw" ("go left"). He carries a bull-whip which he cracks over their heads to tell them which way to go, and sometimes he uses it to flick flies away from their ears, but he never hits them with it. The pioneers considered it very bad to strike the oxen. Like many pioneer farmers, Mr. Larkin has given his oxen names: Dick, Tom, Hob, Sam, Tip, and Dobie.

Above: *Men's boots were made with no distinction between right and left, so they were very large.*

Above: *Matt Belknap likes to shave whenever he gets the chance, in order to show off his dashing mustache. His shaving kit is very precious, as it was one of the few things left to him by his father. Mr. Larkin's beard not only requires little care, but it also gives him extra protection from the sun.*

Below: *A man's felt hat, woollen undershirt and linen trousers.*

Men's Clothes

Like most of the men in the wagon train, Mr. Larkin wears the same clothes day in, day out. Even though it is mid-summer, he wears a long-sleeved flannel shirt with a woolen undershirt beneath and trousers of wool or linen, or a mixture of the two called "linsey-woolsey." Wool, as the guidebooks noted, offered good protection against the midday sun, the rain or any sudden changes in temperature. Denim, which is often associated with the West, came into wide use only after Levi Strauss introduced it in San Francisco in the 1870s. On Mr. Larkin's feet are stout boots that give good protection against snakebite. He also wears a broad-brimmed hat to keep the sun off his head and face – with no sunglasses or sunscreen, this was very important.

Above: *A woman's blouse and sunbonnet.*

"Today mother became very angry with me for removing my sunbonnet. She pointed out to me some girls who did not wear bonnets, and as I did not want to look as brown as an Indian squaw, I put it on again, though it causes me no little discomfort."
Rachel Larkin's Diary

Women's Clothes

Mrs. Larkin walks beside the wagon. Like her husband, she usually dresses in wool, though if the weather is very good she may wear checked gingham. Her skirt is hemmed an inch or two higher than would have been thought proper back East, to make it easier for her to walk over the rough ground. Mrs. Larkin also wears an apron, partly to keep her dress clean, and partly because she, like everyone else at the time, considers the apron to be the right thing for a proper married woman – that is, a housewife – to wear. Although she does not have many clothes for the trip and has few chances for washing, Mrs. Larkin makes a point of wearing a neat, light-colored apron on special occasions (*see page 36*). Her only regret is that she cannot starch it properly, as she would have back in Indiana. She always wears a sunbonnet to protect her face.

Rachel's clothing is much like her mother's, but because of her delicate health she usually rides on horseback, sitting with her skirts carefully pulled down to cover her ankles. Rachel feels envious of the more daring women in the party, who are wearing "bloomers."

Left: *Mr. Larkin bought this fine side-saddle for Rachel in St. Louis.*

Landmarks On The Trail

For the most part, the "trail" was exactly that: A rough, unimproved track. On difficult terrain, the wagons might follow the well-worn ruts left by previous travelers, some of which can still be seen today, but on easier ground, the trail might spread out over a mile or more. There were a few places where army engineers or private businessmen had laid out proper roads by clearing away the trees and boulders. One of the best-known of these was a good road made by Sam Barlow, who charged the overlanders a toll to use it. Most of them paid up willingly, as it saved them having to take a dangerous trip down the falls and rapids of the Columbia.

Left: *A gulch or small valley. There were many of these along the wagon trail. This gulch originally had a stream running through it, but it has dried out.*

Above: *The Rocky Mountains.*

"Today we reached the foot of Chimney Rock. People say that it was thrust up out of the ground, but no one agrees how. One man, who had been a teacher back in Illinois, said that before the Flood the whole land had been as high as that rock." Rachel Larkin's Diary

Right: *The Larkin children are intrigued by the underground cities of the prairie dogs, burrowing owls, and rattlesnakes, like the snake shown here.*

Below: *A hand-drawn map of the trail from an overlander's notebook, with the names of rivers, mountains, and stopping places such as forts.*

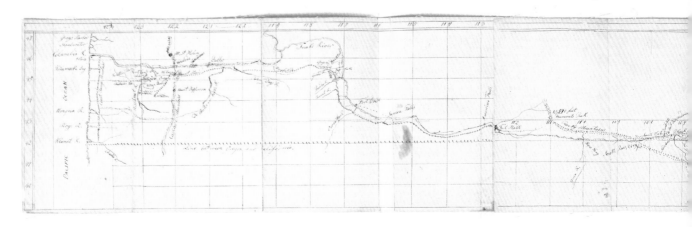

Left: *As the Larkins get farther west, they spot many porcupines. The Indians use porcupine quills to decorate buckskin.*

The Larkins eagerly await their first glimpse of the trail's best-known landmarks, made famous by guidebook descriptions, magazine illustrations, and paintings: the mountains at Scotts Bluff, Laramie Peak, the mountain called Devil's Gate which was almost split in two by a deep notch, and Courthouse Rock and nearby Jail Rock, so called because their shapes reminded some early overlanders of the St. Louis government buildings. There was also Soda Springs, where the bubbling waters tickled the travelers' noses and the bicarbonate deposits gave them new supplies of

Above: *Chimney Rock, painted in 1837.*

Right: *Brown bears were found throughout the Northern Rockies.*

baking soda, and Steamboat Springs, whose puffs and snorts reminded overlanders of river travel back East. Independence Rock was called the "great register of the desert," and travelers climbed it to paint or carve their names. But most famous of all was Chimney Rock (*see left*), a solitary 500-foot spire of sandstone and clay, rising above the flat prairie.

TRIBES OF THE WEST

After they crossed the Missouri, the overlanders were in Indian country. First they encountered the *Oto* and *Kansa* tribes as well as some *Potowatomie* and *Kickapoo*. These Indians lived in villages and bartered their vegetables for items like cloth and fishhooks. They also kept toll bridges over the deeply cut prairie creeks, which the overlanders found helpful but infuriating, as they had to pay to get across.

Left: *A Klickitat Indian. The Klickitat lived in the foothills of the Cascade Mountains and hunted in the Willamette Valley (see map on page 4).*

The *Pawnee* did some farming, but they were also horsemen and hunters. They wore their heads shaved Mohawk style, and frequently fought with other plains tribes over hunting territory. The *Lakota* (or *Dakota*) were a group of tribes whom the overlanders usually called the *Sioux*. Like the *Cheyenne* and *Arapaho*, they had been forced onto the plains in the eighteenth century by rival tribes. They became the most famous of the buffalo-hunting Indians of the plains.

The *Shoshone* Indians hunted, trapped, and fished in the northern mountain regions. Like the *Nez Perce* and *Salish* (*Flatheads*), they were friendly to white people, supplying them with fresh fish and berries and sometimes acting as guides.

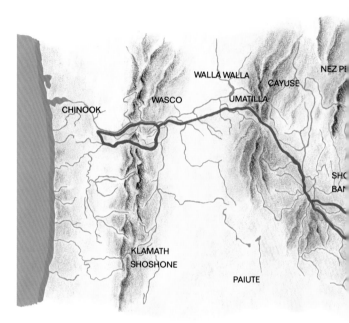

CHINOOK
WASCO
WALLA WALLA
CAYUSE
UMATILLA
NEZ PE
KLAMATH
SHOSHONE
PAIUTE
SHO
BAN

Right: *The tepee had a framework of 16 to 20 poles, lashed together near the top. This supported a semi-circular cover of buffalo hides held in place by foot-long wooden pins slipped through the overlapping holes. The beds were made of pole frames padded with grass and covered with buffalo hides. Backrests made of woven willow were attached to turn them into daytime seating.*

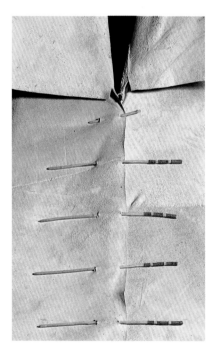

This was so well known that if an Indian from any tribe in the region wanted to show goodwill to an overlander, he would say, "I Shoshone."

In the infertile regions of the Great Basin the *Utes* and related tribes had to live chiefly on roots and plants, which led overlanders bound for California to call them all *Digger* Indians. The *Cayuse, Umatilla, Chinook,* and other fishing tribes whom the Oregon settlers met on the banks of the Columbia were more prosperous.

"Today we saw some Nez Perce Indians. Father tried to say some words to them in their own language, which he got out of Mr. Palmer's Guidebook, but they only laughed and so he walked away." Abe Larkin's Diary

Below: *Map of Indian territory.*

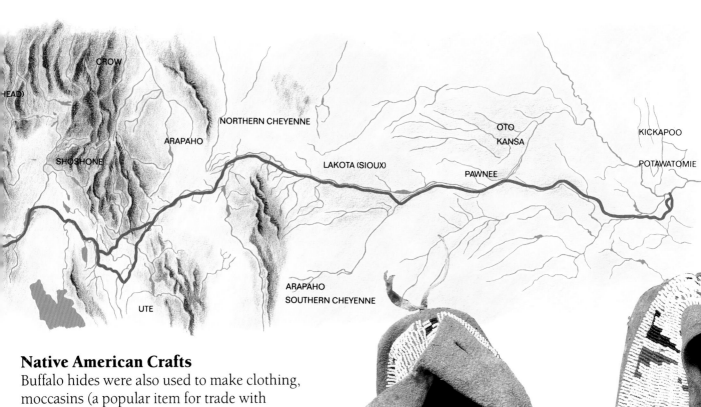

Native American Crafts

Buffalo hides were also used to make clothing, moccasins (a popular item for trade with overlanders), saddles for women (warriors used only a folded blanket secured by a girth!), and parfleches, which were folding traveling pouches. In earlier times, these articles would have been decorated with geometrical designs fashioned from porcupine quills, but from about 1800 porcelain and glass beads, obtained from white traders, began to be used instead.

Right: *Fancy moccasins like these were probably used for ceremonies only. The beads would have been acquired in trade with the whites.*

23

Indian Country

I n the 1840s and early 1850s, the Indians showed little interest in the overlanders. Sometimes the Indians demanded payments or goods, but often they were simply interested in making a good trade. What little bloodshed there was generally involved small bands of young braves out to impress their friends by stealing horses. More often than not, these youngsters were acting against the wishes of the chiefs, who had no desire to anger the travelers. Although the Indians were more a nuisance than a danger, the overlanders were wary. People like the Larkins had thought of Indians as "noble savages," but when they read exaggerated stories about their cruelty in the "penny press," they were worried. The men who

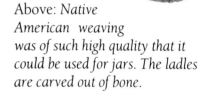

"This afternoon we passed a village of Sioux Indians. The women had moccasins and beads, which they wanted to trade for bread. Husband traded a big Indian a lot of pilot bread for a pair of moccasins, but after we started out he ran up making a big fuss and wanted them back. They had eaten some of the pilot bread and were not satisfied. We handed the moccasins to him in a hurry and drove away as fast as possible." Mrs. Larkin's Diary

Above: *Native American weaving was of such high quality that it could be used for jars. The ladles are carved out of bone.*

guarded the wagon train at night would fire at any noise, and often ended up shooting each other. However, the Indians were much more interested in organizing raids against their traditional enemies than in attacking the overlanders. The Indians often used the rivers to mark the edges of their hunting grounds. As the wagon trains followed the rivers (*see page 32*), overlanders often met up with parties of Indians off to do battle. But they soon realized that, although young braves might steal their animals, the war parties would ignore them completely.

Left: *Native American tomb.*

The Indians' love of children was well known. One diary tells of a mother who put down her baby in some tall grass in order to help her husband lower their wagon down a steep hill. She was horrified to see a band of Indians gathering round her child, and ran toward them. They stood back to let her pass, and she found her child lying as she had left him.

The Indians had been babysitting.

Above: *Native American dress included a blanket and moccasins. The saddle is covered with fur.*

By the mid-1850s, relations between Indians and overlanders had worsened. A series of misunderstandings, and some trigger-happy officers, led to the massacre of a Sioux village after the villagers had been deceived by a flag of truce. This, and other similar conflicts, led to over 30 years of "Indian Wars."

By 1890 the Indians' old way of life had been destroyed. The buffalo, numbering perhaps twelve million in 1850, was nearly extinct, made so by the white hunters armed with their new and very effective breech-loading rifles (*see page 26*). White settlers were farming the prairies and plains and the once mighty tribes of the west were confined to reservations.

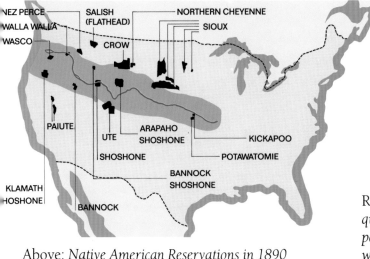

NEZ PERCE
WALLA WALLA
WASCO
SALISH (FLATHEAD)
NORTHERN CHEYENNE
SIOUX
CROW
PAIUTE
UTE
ARAPAHO
SHOSHONE
SHOSHONE
KICKAPOO
POTAWATOMIE
BANNOCK
SHOSHONE
KLAMATH
SHOSHONE
BANNOCK

Above: *Native American Reservations in 1890*

Right: *This hunting quiver, made of animal pelts (skins), is decorated with beads and red cloth.*

HUNTING

The prairies were known to be rich in game, and the overlanders counted on being able to hunt for food. They were well prepared: Each adult male was expected to

Above: *The cartridges in this belt were used by buffalo-hunters with breech-loading rifles.*

have at least one rifle and a revolver. Additional supplies included shotguns, bullet molds, lead, gunpowder, and assorted knives. The guidebooks

advised overlanders to carry these weapons in case they were attacked by Indians, but in fact they were used far more often for hunting. Each morning the captain would send out a well-armed party of sharp-shooters like Matt Belknap, to hunt.

During the first stages of the journey the hunters seldom came back with anything bigger than rabbits, prairie chickens, pheasants, and other small birds and animals. But as they traveled farther west, they could hope for elk, antelope, bighorn sheep, and, best of all, buffalo.

Techniques for hunting buffalo varied. Before they got horses and firearms, the Indians would often stampede a herd over a precipice and then finish them off with bows and arrows. A hunter armed with a rifle might walk to within a few yards of a buffalo, and if it did not catch his scent, he could fire off round after round of bullets.

Above: *A buffalo-hunter's kit, with a warm jacket, cartridge bag, and saddle.*

Right: *A professional buffalo-hunter at work. Much of the equipment used by hunters was bought from the army.*

Left: *A hunting knife.*

"The valley of the Platte is dotted all over with the skeletons of buffalo. Such waste of creatures that God has made for man seems wicked, but every emigrant seems to wish to signalize himself by killing one." Mrs. Larkin's Diary

The buffalo, which could be up to ten feet long, and weigh as much as a ton, would simply stand there with a dazed expression and then drop to the ground, stone dead. More adventurous hunters might ride into the flank of a stampeding herd, single out one buffalo, and aim for the spine in hopes of felling it with a single shot.

Right: A hunting pouch, a horn powder flask, and two guns. The top one is a shotgun used for small game, and the bottom one is a muzzle-loading rifle for heavier game such as antelope. Below them is a powder keg.

Above: An American pheasant.

Below: Shooting equipment: a powder flask, bullet mold, and gun lock. To make round musket balls for his rifle, Matt Belknap pours lead into the mold through the hole at the top and waits for it to solidify before opening it up again.

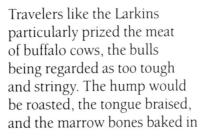

Travelers like the Larkins particularly prized the meat of buffalo cows, the bulls being regarded as too tough and stringy. The hump would be roasted, the tongue braised, and the marrow bones baked in the coals of the campfire. Meat that was not eaten fresh would be preserved by the traditional Indian technique of jerking. Cut into thin strips, it would hang over a smokey fire for half a day or dangle from the back of the wagon to cure. If there was time, the hide would be cured, so that eventually a pile of robes might lie alongside the family's store of blankets.

Early overlanders like the Larkins tried to use as much of the buffalo as possible, just as the Indians did. But as overland travel became more common, this changed. The earliest overlanders reported seeing the plains black with buffalo and they lived in fear of a deadly stampede. Within a few decades, however, as more and more overlanders killed for "sport" rather than for needed food, and commercial hunters killed for the hides, the once-vast herds were nearly exterminated. By then overlanders had other food sources, but the Indians had lost their traditional hunting forever.

CHILDREN'S ACTIVITIES

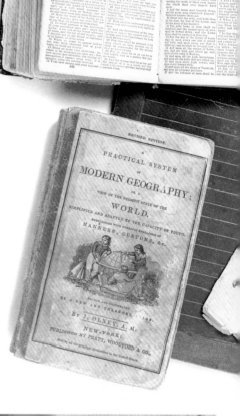

For the Larkin children, the journey to Oregon began as one great holiday. "We're going to where the Injuns be!" shouted Abe when his father told him their plans. Of course, they had chores to do each day – milking the cows, carrying water – just as they did back in Indiana. But Abe would not be helping his father with the plowing, and Rachel and Rebecca would not be doing spinning, quilting, and other household chores alongside their mother. Back in Indiana, Rachel, Abe and Rebecca went to school, at least for most of the winter months. Older pupils like Rachel did lessons in grammar and geography from textbooks, and younger ones would "work out" sums on a slate, practice handwriting in their copybooks, or recite in turn from a reader. But there is no time for formal "schooling" on the trail, although Mrs. Larkin or one of the other mothers sometimes holds a spelling bee or hears the children recite.

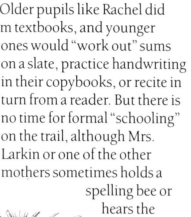

Above: *Rabbitbrush grows in the drier regions of the west. It has yellow blossoms and a very strong smell.*

Right: *Fir cone.*

The Larkin children gather berries, currants, and hazelnuts. They pick wild flowers: Black-eyed Susans, purple blazing star, wild geraniums, and the pink prairie rose. Sometimes they find a species they have never seen before, so they save some seeds to plant in Oregon or send to friends back East. But the children soon get tired of the journey. Rebecca complains of dust or mud, depending on the weather. Mrs. Larkin keeps little Margaret happy by giving her some colored beads to string together – a difficult task in a bouncing wagon.

Above: *Margaret tries to catch lizards, but they are always too quick for her.*

"Matthew brought me some flowers... Their form and color resemble the snowball and their perfume the night-blooming jessamine."
Rachel Larkin's Diary

NOONING

I t is midday, and the wagons have been rolling along for five hours. The day is hot and the oxen are tired.

Captain Bonner's advance scouts have found a cool stream not far ahead, and he calls a halt. The wagons pull up and the oxen are released, though not unyoked, and the whole party settles down for an hour of rest.

Above: *Overlanders resting beside their wagons at noon.*

Above:
Mr. and Mrs. Larkin followed the guidebook's advice to "lay in a good supply of school books for the children."

"Mrs. Pringle called on me today and very much admired my bonnet. I promised to give her the pattern and returned the compliment by admiring her apron."
Mrs. Larkin's Diary

"Nooning" is Mrs. Larkin's favorite time of day. The family eat leftovers from breakfast, so she does not have to do any cooking.

Little Margaret, whom she has been carrying on her hip all morning, is allowed to toddle about and play, the older children run off to see their friends in the other wagons, and Mr. Larkin leaves for a meeting with Captain Bonner and his council.

Mrs. Larkin uses the time to relax and to write in her diary. She notes down the latest gossip on the wagon train, and any news she has been able to get of the outside world.

Below: *Abe's fishing gear has a collapsible rod which is ideal for travel. He is disappointed by the lack of fishing on the high plains, but there are catfish in the slow, muddy waters of the Big Blue and trout and salmon in the rivers of the western mountains.*

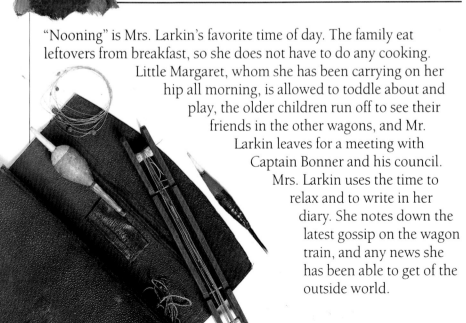

MISHAPS

From 1852 to 1853, almost 90,000 overlanders headed for Oregon and California. The wagon trains, which left the jumping-off points almost daily, often overtook each other. They also met up with "go-backers" who were returning east. They had "seen the elephant" (*see left*), an expression meaning that they had experienced the hardships of life in the west and decided they could not put up with them. Besides the weariness of months of travel, the overlanders had many other problems: Even if the driver was as good as Mr. Larkin, any wagon, however well made, could break down, and the oxen could become sick or exhausted (*see below*).

Above: Crossing the Plains, *1851. Painting by Charles Nahl.*

"Alkali water" killed many oxen. This water was full of chemical salts left behind as the lakes dried out in the hot weather. An ox that had drunk this water might be saved if chunks of bacon and swigs of vinegar could be forced down its throat to stop the salts burning its insides. Rough ground and desert sands were also a hazard, as they often led to lameness and sore feet. The remedy for this was to put the ox in booties made of rawhide.

"There is no end to the wagons, buggies, yokes, chains, etc. that are lying all along this road, and many the poor horses, mules, oxen, cows, etc. that are lying dead in these mountains." Mrs. Larkin's Diary

Above: *There were other hazards besides sick oxen. A broken wheel was almost irreplaceable. Few wagon trains had time to wait while a new wheel was made out of a discarded table top or some other piece of quality furniture.*

Right: *A "brake" made of strong rope stopped the wheels turning.*

Broken axles were taken almost as a matter of course. Nearly every wagon started out with at least one spare, to reduce the risk of having to detour for miles in search of a tree large enough to be made into a replacement.

The iron tires on the wagon wheels sometimes became loose as the wooden wheels shrank in the dry desert air, and they had to be held in place by wedges.

Left: *Almost every overlander was obliged to abandon some valued objects, ranging from cook-stoves to barrels of bacon and boxes of books, in order to lighten their load. One overlander even saw an abandoned diving bell!*

Difficult Terrain

Mountain slopes and steep hills presented a challenge, even to the most experienced driver. It was relatively easy to go uphill, as the oxen were used to pulling, and they could be double-teamed. If the going was very hard, a makeshift windlass could be set up: An empty wagon was staked on the hilltop, with one set of wheels running free, and a strong rope tied to that axle was lowered to the wagon below. Then the men and oxen would slowly turn the wheels, reeling the wagon up the hill like a fish. Going downhill was more difficult, as oxen were not used to braking. Rope "brakes" could be used to lock the wheels, but this did not always stop the wagon sliding down the hill and being damaged. Even the gently rolling plains could cause problems for an inexperienced driver, as the top-heavy wagons tipped over easily.

Left: *Tool box for wagon repairs.*

CROSSING A RIVER

The wagon trail followed the course of rivers, which were important because they provided water and grass. However, they had to be crossed again and again, often with some difficulty. By the time of the Larkins' journey, there were many ferries. They made crossing safer and easier, but heavy traffic on the trail sometimes created delays of several days, and prices were high. If there was no bridge or ferry – or if the overlander did not have enough money to use them – he could simply drive his

wagon across the river or stream at its shallowest spot, with his family inside.

Mr. Larkin, whose guidebooks were out-of-date, had not expected the extra expense, so he usually makes the livestock swim across and puts only the wagon on the ferry. He is annoyed by the delay of waiting for the ferry, but Mrs. Larkin is delighted to have a chance to do the laundry. Lacking firewood, she and Rachel must make do with cold water and lots of strong soap. The soap was homemade, from a liquid called lye which was got from ashes and animal fat.

After a thorough rubbing, the clothing is rinsed, wrung out, and hung on any available bushes to dry. If there are no bushes, it may simply be put on wet.

"Mother and I burnt our arms very badly while washing. They were red and swollen and painful as though scalded with boiling water." Rachel Larkin's Diary

Above: *Good fords were not always easy to find. Hidden boulders or quicksand could wreck a wagon, like the abandoned one shown here, or it might overturn in a tricky current.*

Below: *If the water was too deep to drive across, there was no alternative but to tow the wagon across with the swimming cattle, as this painting shows. Mr. Larkin usually asks Matt to ride ahead of the wagon and look out for any dangers.*

The Thomas Gilcrease Institute of American History and Art, Tulsa, Oklahoma

32

DISASTER

Rumors of disaster spread quickly, and the Larkins would have heard of the fates of overlanders such as the Donner Party. This wagon train was full of rich families, who left their jumping-off point at the end of May 1846 a month late, because they were kitting out wagons with fancy things. They exhausted their oxen trying to catch up with the rest of the overlanders, and took a short-cut recommended in Lansford Hasting's guidebook. The author wanted to make the route seem easy, but he had not even tried it himself! Making only one or two miles a day in the grassless salt desert, the party was forced to abandon most of its animals. By the time the wagons reached the foothills of the Sierra Nevada, snow had blocked the mountain passes and it was too late to turn back. The families had to spend the winter there, in crude log cabins. By mid-December the party was starving and 17 members tried to cross the mountains to get help (*see left*). Seven of this party made it to Sutter's Fort, where a rescue operation was begun. After two failed attempts, a rescue party finally reached them in April 1847. Only 47 of the original 81 people were alive. Many had survived only by eating their dead companions.

The Donner Party was not the only one to run into trouble. Stephen Meek persuaded his party to take a completely new route in order to avoid the Blue Mountains. They ended up lost, with no grass or water. Meek went ahead by himself and managed to reach the Columbia River. A rescue party was organized, but they found that 75 people had already died.

If such disasters were rare, it was because overlanders learned from

Above: Lansford W. Hasting's misleading guidebook.

others' mistakes. Virginia Reed, a survivor of the Donner party, had some good advice for anyone thinking of making the journey: "Never take no cut offs and hurry along as fast as you can."

STOPPING AT A FORT

Before setting out from Independence, the Larkins followed the guidebooks' instructions closely, as they wanted to have enough supplies for the whole trip. However, not all emigrants were so careful, and even those who had packed properly often found they needed extra supplies, so they were very glad of the forts and trading posts along the way.

Right: A painting of Fort Laramie and the surrounding Indian village by Alfred Jacob Miller.

Left: A photographer has set up shop at the fort, and people have pictures taken to send to their relatives.

Fort Laramie

The Larkins' party has arrived at Fort Laramie, which by 1853 had become a bustling trading post. This fort was established by the American Fur Company in 1834 to buy animal pelts brought in by "mountain men" and Indian trappers (*see opposite page*). By the 1840s, the fur trade had declined, and as the numbers of overlanders had grown, it was realized that more money could be made from selling them goods and offering much-needed services such as a post office, a hospital, and a blacksmith. The sutler, or army provisioner, who supplied the troops with food from his shop also sold goods to the overlanders.

Many people felt that soldiers should be stationed along the wagon trails to protect overlanders against attacks by Indians, and by the 1850s, 90 percent of the U.S. Army was stationed in the West. The army bought Fort Laramie from the American Fur Company for $4,000 in 1849 and it became the first and most important in a string of military garrisons.

Above: *The sign outside the sutler's store boasts that it stocks "all articles a man wants in civilized countries or on the plains."*

"We are thankful that our bacon has kept, as supplies here are very dear. Five dollars won't buy what a dollar bought back East."
Mrs. Larkin's Diary

Fort Laramie a Sublettes Fort near the Nebraska a Platte River

Although the sight of the cavalry's blue coats made the overlanders feel safe, the army was not really very good at protecting them. Reports of problems with Indians could take days to reach a fort, and sometimes the cavalry's response would be to attack the wrong Indians, which caused more fighting and made the Indians mistrustful of the army and the overlanders. The government's Indian agents, who arranged peace treaties with various Indian tribes in exchange for annual payments, were far more effective than the soldiers. However, the army and the Indians were not completely hostile to one another: Villages of Indians, eager to trade, usually encircled the walls of the stockades.

Right: *Some of the furs traded in the early days at Fort Laramie: Deer, red fox, ermine, river otter, and buffalo.*

Left: *Infantryman in uniform.*

Above: *Cavalryman's saddle, curry combs and canteen.*

Right: *A soldier's winter overcoat and belt with a powder pouch, bullet bag, and pistol. Cavalrymen usually carried their pistols in holsters, like the ones shown here, slung over the fronts of their saddles.*

A SPECIAL DAY

Only rarely did the Larkins and their company take time off for a celebration. Even Sunday, the "Sabbath" of these normally religious people, would pass like any other day, unless they encountered a traveling

Above: *The family Bible.*

preacher. People said, "There's no Sunday west of Kansas." Weddings, however, did call for special activity. The couple would be subjected to a "chivaree," as their friends spent the wedding night jostling their wagon, shooting off guns, and banging on kettles. Overlanders tended to marry young, especially girls. It was unusual for a girl not to be married by the age of 16.

Right: *Preparations for the Independence Day celebrations.*

Only one special day is regularly mentioned in the overlanders' diaries: The Fourth of July, Independence Day. The Larkins and their company are especially pleased because they have reached Independence Rock, so named by a group of early travelers who reached it on Independence Day. This means that, despite the rainy weather, they are right on schedule. They spend a few days on the grassy banks of the Sweetwater River, grazing their oxen and celebrating their good fortune.

The Fourth of July Feast

The sideboards of the wagons are laden with antelope, sagehen, and rabbit, both roasted and fried, several kinds of fresh bread, baked beans, rice, and, as a special treat, Irish potatoes and pickled cucumbers brought all the way from Missouri. To drink, there is coffee, tea, and "lemonade" made of sugar, water, citric acid, and a few drops of essence of lemon. Over a dozen sorts of cakes and pies are spread out for dessert, and some long-hoarded chocolate is given to the children.

Matt and Rachel join a group of young people who climb Independence Rock

Above: *It was a tradition for the travelers to sign their names on Independence Rock.*

to look for the names of friends and to write their own. Meanwhile, Mrs. Larkin and the other women have decided that, to celebrate properly, they need an American flag. One of them has some scraps of blue cloth, another has red, and another white. By the time the party begins, Old Glory, complete with 28 stars, flies from a makeshift flagpole in the middle of the wagon circle. Many of the company are dressed up in costume. Rachel is decked out as "Lady Liberty," but most of the young people are dressed as Indians. The "Indians" perform "war dances" to the delight of the crowd.

There is a contest to see which of the children can best remember the Declaration of Independence from their school days back east, with the winner to receive the last precious piece of chocolate. The "official" party closes with three cheers for America (Oregon Territory in particular) and a five-gun salute, but the dancing and revelling go on late into the night.

Right: *Pen-box, inkwell, and spectacles. Steel tipped pens began replacing quills in the late 1820s.*

As always, Mrs. Larkin writes a detailed account of the celebration in her diary. Many overlanders kept diaries, and a lot of them still survive. Some, like Mr. Larkin's, have short entries: "June 20. Up Platte River. Good road. Made 21 mi. June 29. Up same. Overtook Capt. Tutherew's Company. Made 15 mi." Others, like Mrs. Larkin's and Rachel's, contain more interesting information.

SICKNESS & DEATH

O f nearly 300,000 emigrants who headed west between 1840 and 1860, around 30,000, or one in ten, died along the way. Some diaries speak of practically nothing but death and burial. Accidents accounted for the deaths of some of the overlanders. Diary accounts tell of little children falling out of wagons and being crushed beneath the wheels, of people being shot by night guards who mistook them for Indians trying to steal their livestock, and of men being swept away and drowned when they tried to herd their cattle across raging rivers.

Left: *A wooden tombstone like this was unusual. Most graves were simply mounds of earth.*

Above: Prairie Burial, *c. 1848. Painting by William Tylee Ranney. Even if a person was in the best of health, a serious attack of cholera could kill in a single day.*

"July 11. Passed 15 graves. Made 13 mi. July 12. Passed 5 graves. Saw 8 dead cattle. Made 10 mi."
Mr. Larkin's Diary

However, the most common cause of death on the trail was disease: Measles, typhoid, mountain fever, the "bloody flux," or dysentery, and above all the dreaded cholera. Asiatic cholera, carried by rats on ships, arrived in American port cities in late 1848 and 1849 and from there it spread to anywhere with poor water supplies and bad plumbing. Even cities such as St. Louis lost a tenth of their population, and the wagon trains, who were camping and watering every day with no proper toilets, in the same places as all the previous trains had camped, were particularly hard hit by the disease.

Like most overlanders, the Larkins have a variety of medicines: Laudanum (tincture of opium) and camphor for cholera, hartshorne for snakebites, citric acid for scurvy, castor oil for bowel disorders, borax and alum for boils and sores, and whiskey and various dried herbs for everything else.

Doctors
If someone was very ill, the party might try to summon a doctor. Often traveling by wagon train themselves, doctors advertised their services and let people know where they were by posting notices on the "roadside telegraph." Their fees varied considerably. Some took payment only for medicines, while others charged a fee for visiting the patient. Typical charges might be $2 for seeing a cholera

victim and up to $5 for an amputation or for setting a broken limb.

But even doctors knew little about the cause and prevention of cholera. It was not until 1865 that Louis Pasteur demonstrated that germs cause diseases like cholera. The doctors did know that dirty water was associated with the disease, but they did not realize that boiling the water would kill the deadly germs. It is very lucky for the Larkins that they like to drink strong boiled coffee with every meal. This makes them much less likely to catch cholera.

Even overlanders like the Larkins who remained fairly healthy still had the never-ending nuisance of mosquito bites to put up with. It was common for people to be bitten so many times that their blood stopped being able to clot.

Above:
Advertisement for cholera remedies.

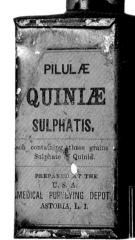

Left: *A portable medical case.*

Right: *Quinine was used to treat the disease malaria, which overlanders caught from mosquito bites.*

"So many of our company have died of the cholera that I cannot recount all their names. The burials have been at night on account of Indians robbing the graves for wearing apparel. The graves are concealed by building a fire on them and then driving the entire train of wagons over them when we break camp in the morning."
Mrs. Larkin's Diary

Right: *Setting up camp for the night*

Above:
*Mrs. Larkin decides
not to light a lantern. Her candles
have to last until she arrives in
Oregon and can make more.*

SETTING UP CAMP

R ain and heavy trail traffic have made it hard to find good campsites this year, and sometimes the Larkins' wagon train has traveled late into the night before reaching a suitable place. Today, however, Captain Bonner's advance scouts have had no trouble. At 6pm the bugle sounds. Captain Bonner lays out some stakes to help him guide the train into a neat circle. He is so accurate that the last wagon closes the circle perfectly. The operation has taken only ten minutes.

Mr. Larkin and Matt Belknap unyoke the oxen and drive them to pasture near a waterhole. Then they water the horses. Finally, just inside the wagon circle, they set up the little wall tent in which Rachel, Abe, and Rebecca will sleep. Mr. and Mrs. Larkin and Margaret will sleep on featherbeds inside the wagon. Matt will sleep in the open, though if it rains he will roll under the wagon.

*"O dear, I do so want to get there! It is now
two months since we have slept in a house. If only I
could be set down at home with all the folks…"*
Mrs. Larkin's Diary

Above: *The children have been
gathering up buffalo chips for the
fire. They have to get enough to
cook supper and breakfast.*

Above: *Hobbles like the one shown are used to tie the horses to the wagon at night.*

Right: *A folding camp chair makes dining much more comfortable.*

The family will be eating cornbread and beans, fried meat and gravy – the basic diet of the overlander. But there will be warm milk, fresh from the cow, to drink, and Mrs. Larkin and Rebecca have found enough berries to make a pie, which will be baked in the old dutch oven.

The able-bodied men of the party have been divided into three companies, each split into four watches. One company has to guard the wagon train each night, its first watch waking members of the second watch, and so on through the night. It is just 8pm when the first watch takes up its duties.

ENTERTAINMENT

On the high plains the overlanders went to bed early, there being little fuel for fires. But elsewhere, they gathered together to chat about the day's travel. Some men played dice or cards, but others thought that gambling was sinful. Some people even thought that playing chess was wicked.

Whiskey is also frowned upon, although many overlanders, especially gold miners, did drink. On the Larkins' wagon train, it is used "for medicinal purposes only." Dancing and singing, however, are enjoyed by everyone. Songs about home, love, and death are popular, as are funny songs like "Oh Susanna."

It is midnight when the fiddler stops playing, but the Larkins are already in bed and asleep. Matt Belknap, on the watch, is still awake. He gazes up at the stars and thinks about Oregon.

Above: *The Larkins' party is lucky to have a melodeon or "American organ," as well as fiddles and harmonicas. They plan to have a "cotillion" or square dance, with visitors from a nearby wagon train.*

OREGON AT LAST

The Larkins arrive in Oregon City on September 10, 1853, four months after leaving Independence and nearly five months after leaving Indiana. On the last stages of their journey two of their oxen died and had to be replaced by milk cows, but they themselves have all survived to see "civilization" once more. They spend a few days shopping for food and catching up on the latest news of Oregon and the world. While prices are higher than in St. Louis, they are at least lower than on the trail.

Left: *Building a log cabin.*

Above: *Oregon City as it looked in 1848. Painting by Henry J. Warre.*

Coffee, for example, is selling for 18 cents a pound and fresh beef for 4 to 6 cents.

Soon the Larkins are on the move again, this time for the short journey to the less developed regions of the upper Willamette valley to claim their new land. No one is surprised when Matt Belknap asks Rachel to marry him. They will also be given land under the terms of the 1850 Donation Land Act (*see page 6*).

(*see page 6*).

Below: *Tin washtubs hang on the outside of the Larkins' new cabin.*

Left: *The* Daily Portland Times *advertises livestock sales, saloons, and job opportunities.*

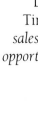

Mrs. Larkin can be proud of. A new stove will provide heat, and a flatiron will allow her to press her treasured fancy aprons and calico frocks.

Bountiful crops of grain and hops – as well as clean mountain water – will provide the raw material for brewing beer. The Larkins will do well in Oregon, a land not exactly flowing with milk and honey but prosperous nonetheless.

Above: *Mrs. Larkin will have little chance to spin in Oregon, as there are very few sheep. A few women tried spinning hair from wolves but as these animals cannot be fleeced while alive, it was not very practical. Most people relied either on "store-bought" cloth or wore buckskin like the mountain men.*

Above right: *A candle mold. Although there is not much beeswax, there is plenty of tallow, so Mrs. Larkin can make candles.*

Left: *Supplies carried in the wagon are at last stored in the Larkins' new log cabin. Included are an iron wood-burning stove, canteens, irons, and pots and pans. There is also an accordion and the latest edition of a local newspaper.*

Below: *Mrs. Larkin uses a basket and bottles for storage.*

Settling In

With no summer crops to live on and little money left, the Larkins have a hard first winter in Oregon, but with their neighbors' help, they survive. Mr. Larkin raises a log cabin. Even the chimney is wooden, but fortunately it is well plastered with mud on the inside to reduce the risk of fire. Mr. Larkin cannot afford to install window glass yet: That costs $6 for a small box. Neither can he construct a proper shingle roof: That would take too much time. Instead, he puts up a rough frame and covers it with canvas from the wagon top. A buffalo hide serves as the door. The wagon box is broken up for furniture. The Larkins' "Hoosier Home" has become part of their new home in Oregon. Within a few years, it will be transformed into something that even

"I am thankful that we have at last reached Oregon. The land is better than we had hoped, and our prospects are bright." Mr. Larkin's Diary

THE WAGON IN TIME

The Larkin family traveled from Indiana to Oregon in 1853. Here are some of the things that took place in the United States and around the world before, during, and after the Larkins made their journey.

1800 Population of the United States recorded as 5,308,483.

1803 The United States buys the lands between the Mississippi and the Rocky Mountains from France for $15,000,000, doubling the size of the nation.

1804-1806 The Lewis and Clark Expedition explores the upper Missouri and Oregon territory.

1805-1807 Zebulon Pike searches for the source of the Mississippi and explores the Rocky mountains.

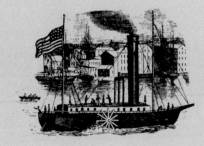

1807 Engineer Robert Fulton develops the first practical steamboat.

1811 John Jacob Astor establishes a trading post in Oregon.

1812-1814 War between the United States and Great Britain.

1816 The state of Indiana is admitted to the union.

1818 The United States and Great Britain agree to joint occupancy of Oregon country.

1819 The United States buys Florida from Spain.

1820 Death of frontiersman Daniel Boone at age 85.

1821-1824 Wars of independence end Spanish colonial rule in Mexico and South America.

1828 The first American railroad, the Baltimore and Ohio, begins operation. Andrew Jackson, advocate of western expansion, is elected president of the United States.

1830 Joseph Smith founds the Mormon Church (Latter Day Saints).
Congress passes the Indian Removal Act, giving President Jackson the power to remove Native Americans from the east to lands west of the Mississippi.

1832 *Godey's Lady's Book* begins publication. A popular magazine, it introduced women to the latest fashions and literature.

1833 John Deere patents the steel plow, which, unlike the older cast-iron plow, can turn over the heavy turf of the Western prairies.

1834 Cyrus McCormick patents the reaper.

1835 Samuel Colt patents his six-shooter revolver.

1836 The Lone Star Republic (now Texas) becomes independent from Mexico.
Marcus and Narcissa Whitman establish a Methodist mission in Oregon Country.

1837 Accession of Queen Victoria in Great Britain.

1838 French inventor Louis Daguerre develops the first practical photographic process, producing "daguerreotypes."

1842-1845 John Frémont maps the west.

1843 First wagon train crosses to Oregon.
Samuel Morse's electromagnetic telegraph operates between Washington and Baltimore.

1844 James K. Polk elected president of the United States on a slogan of "50°40' or Fight" ("All of Oregon or War.")

1845 The Lone Star Republic enters the union as the state of Texas. In his *Democratic Review* John L. O'Sullivan writes of the United States' "Manifest Destiny" to expand across the Continent.

1846 California becomes independent from Mexico as the Bear Flag Republic.
The Donner Party disaster.

1847 Oregon Boundary Treaty divides the territory between the United States and Great Britain at 49° north latitude.
Marcus and Narcissa Whitman and 12 other settlers are massacred by a group of Cayuse Indians at their mission in Oregon.
Brigham Young leads the Mormons from Nauvoo, Illinois, to Utah.

1848 War with Mexico results in the Mexican cession of California and the Southwest to the United States.
Gold is discovered in California, leading to the 1849-50 gold rush.

1850 The Donation Land Act is passed in the United States. Irish immigration after the Potato Famine passes 160,000 per year. *Harper's Monthly* begins publication in the United States, offering English novels in serial form and illustrated articles about the west.

1852 Harriet Beecher Stowe's novel *Uncle Tom's Cabin* attacks slavery.

1853 The United States acquires southern New Mexico and Arizona from Mexico by the Gadsden Purchase.

The Larkin family emigrate to Oregon.

1854 The Kansas–Nebraska Act formally opens these territories to white settlement and sparks new national debate on slavery.

1859 First oil well, in Pennsylvania, leads to the development of the petroleum industry. Comstock Lode (silver) discovered in Nevada.

1860 First Pony Express delivers letters from St. Louis, Missouri, to Sacramento, California, in 10 days. Population of the United States reaches 31,500,000. Abraham Lincoln is elected president of the United States.

1861-1865 American Civil War.

1861 Telegraph line completed between San Francisco and St. Louis. Emperor Alexander II of Russia emancipates the serfs.

1862 Homestead Act encourages settlement of unoccupied western lands.

1863 Lincoln's Emancipation Proclamation frees the slaves.

1864 Death of Stephen Foster, composer of "Old Kentucky Home" and "The Camptown Races," at age 38.

1865 Lincoln assassinated. French scientist Louis Pasteur publishes his "germ theory" of disease.

1866 First successful transatlantic telegraph cable.

1867 The United States buys Alaska from Russia for $7,200,000. Swedish inventor Alfred Nobel develops dynamite. George Henry Hammond produces the first railway refrigerator car.

1869 The first American transcontinental railroad is completed. The first professional baseball team is organized, in Cincinnati.

1872 First national park is established as the Yellowstone National Park.

1874 Barbed wire is patented. Economical fencing and the introduction of "winter wheat" encourages development of farming on the Great Plains. Alexander Graham Bell demonstrates the telephone.

1875 Gold rush onto Sioux lands leads to the Battle of Little Big Horn ("Custer's Last Stand") in 1876.

1877 Chief Joseph of the Nez Perce surrenders to the U.S. Cavalry. Thomas A. Edison invents the phonograph.

1879 Thomas A. Edison demonstrates the electric light.

1882 The first commercial system of electrification is put in operation in New York City.

1883 The first ten-story "skyscraper" is built in Chicago.

1884 Inventor Hiram Maxim perfects the machine gun.

1886 First manufacture of Coca-Cola.

1888 Scotsman John Dunlop invents the pneumatic tire. American George Eastman perfects the hand camera.

1889 Two million acres of Indian Territory (Oklahoma) are opened to white homesteaders.

1890 Battle of Wounded Knee, ending the western "Indian Wars." Population of the United States reaches 63,000,000 as 450,000 immigrants arrive annually.

GLOSSARY

Bloomers Full, loose trousers, gathered round the ankle, which were introduced by the social reformer Amelia Jenks Bloomer in 1850 because they were more practical for women to wear than long, trailing skirts.

Brave An Indian (Native American) warrior. Among the Native Americans of the Plains, boys had to prove their bravery and strength at hunting and warfare in order to be called braves, and they often competed with each other for the top position. The highest ranking braves of the tribe were the chiefs, who were highly honored, as were the shamans or "medicine men," who had spiritual power. While young boys were taught to become braves, girls were taught home-making skills such as sewing by their mothers and the other women of the tribe, who were called "squaws."

Buckskin Soft leather made from the hide of deer or elk, so named because a male deer is called a "buck."

Buffalo Robe A blanket made from the full hide of a buffalo, tanned with the hair still on it in order to give extra warmth.

Calico A kind of cotton cloth, printed with a figured pattern.

Cholera A short-lasting, often fatal infection caused by drinking or eating water, milk, or food contaminated with bacteria. The symptoms are diarrhea, vomiting, and stomach pains, followed by collapse from loss of water and salt.

Dutch Oven A heavy cast-iron pot with a tight-fitting cover. When heaped with coals, it can be used for baking as well as for stewing.

Dysentery A common trail disease whose symptoms include fatigue, nausea, and diarrhea followed by loss of water and salt.

Emigrant A person who leaves their native country or region to live elsewhere. The early overlanders were called emigrants because they left the settled parts of the United States to go and live in lands in the west which were only just being acquired by the U.S. government.

Forty-Niner A person who went to California looking for gold during the 1849 gold rush.

Gingham A cotton fabric, often with a striped or checked pattern.

Indian Agent A representative of the United States government who served as ambassador to Indian tribes.

Johnnycake A type of bread made of cornmeal mixed with salt and water or milk, which could be either baked in a pan or fried on a griddle.

Manifest Destiny The idea that a nation (such as the United States) must expand until it fills up certain natural geographic limits (e.g., the American continent from the Atlantic ocean to the Pacific ocean).

Mormon A member of the Church of Jesus Christ of Latter-Day Saints, which was a religious group founded by Joseph Smith in 1830. After being driven out of settlements in the East because of religious intolerance, many Mormons, under the leadership of Brigham Young, emigrated to the place that would, in 1846, become the state of Utah.

Mountain Fever A general name given to several diseases which emigrants sometimes caught on the western parts of the Oregon Trail. The symptoms included chills, fever, and extreme fatigue. Mountain fever was weakening, but rarely fatal.

Mountain Men Professional trappers of animals for fur who hunted in the mountain ranges. As more and more emigrants came west, these men were often paid to serve as wagon train guides or "pilots."

Penny Press Publishing companies that sold cheap mini-novels and short stories, which were often very sensational.

Pilot Bread Also known as "hardtack," this was a hard biscuit made from flour and water. As it would keep for a long time, it was commonly used for long journeys by both land and sea.

Prairie The wide, rolling land of the Missouri–Mississippi valley. It had almost no trees, but very deep, rich soil and enough rain for good crops of grain. On its west side, the prairie merges with the high plains, where a lack of rainfall makes the land more suitable for grazing animals than for growing crops.

Rawhide Untanned leather, usually without hair, that has been cured by being stretched and dried.

Scurvy People get this disease when they do not have enough ascorbic acid, which is found in foods such as lemons and limes. The symptoms include loose teeth, and bleeding, painful gums.

Spelling Bee A spelling contest. Contestants are given words to spell out loud. The contest ends when all but one of the participants has failed to spell a word correctly.

Tallow Animal fat which has been purified by melting. It was usually made into candles or mixed up with grease and used to keep the wagon wheels running smoothly.

Typhoid A highly infectious and often fatal disease caused by bacteria. The symptoms are fever, diarrhea, headaches, and, in the later stages, confusion and hemorrhaging of blood.

INDEX

PLACES TO VISIT

The following museums and historic sites have displays on aspects of life on the wagon trail:

DONNER MEMORIAL STATE PARK AND
EMIGRANT TRAIL MUSEUM
12593 Donner Pass Road, Truckee, California 95734
Tel: 916/578-3841

EASTERN OREGON MUSEUM ON THE OLD OREGON TRAIL
Third and Wilcox, Haines, Oregon 97833
Tel: 503/856-3233

FORT LARAMIE NATIONAL HISTORIC SITE
P.O. Box 86, Fort Laramie, Wyoming 82212
Tel: 307/837-2221

GREAT PLAINS BLACK MUSEUM
2213 Lake Street, Omaha, Nebraska 68110
Tel: 402/345-2212

THE HIGH DESERT MUSEUM
59800 South Highway 97, Bend, Oregon 97702-8933
Tel: 503/382-4754

JEFFERSON NATIONAL EXPANSION MEMORIAL/MUSEUM OF
WESTWARD EXPANSION
11 North Fourth Street, St. Louis, Missouri 63102
Tel: 314/425-4468

NEVADA COUNTY HISTORICAL SOCIETY MUSEUM
P.O. Box 1300, Nevada City, California 95959
Tel: 916/265-5468

OREGON HISTORICAL SOCIETY MUSEUM
1230 South West Park Avenue, Portland, Oregon 97205
Tel: 503/222-1741

OREGON TRAIL MUSEUM/SCOTTS BLUFF NATIONAL
MONUMENT
P.O. Box 427, Gering, Nebraska 69341
Tel: 308/436-4340

PIONEER FARM MUSEUM
7716 Ohop Valley Road, Eatonville, Washington 98328
Tel: 206/832-6300

PIONEER HERITAGE CENTER
Highway 5, Cavalier, North Dakota 58220
Tel: 701/265-4561

PIONEER MUSEUM
430 West Fourth Street, Ashland, Kansas 67831
Tel: 316/635-2227

PIONEER MUSEUM
300 East Main Street, Trinidad, Colorado 81082
Tel: 719/846-7217

PIONEER VILLAGE
Box N, Farmington, Utah 84025
Tel: 801/292-2379

SANTA FE TRAIL CENTER/FORT LARNED NATIONAL
HISTORIC SITE
Route 3, Larned, Kansas 67550
Tel: 316/285-6911

WILLA CATHER HISTORICAL CENTER/NEBRASKA STATE
HISTORICAL SOCIETY
338 North Webster Road, Red Cloud, Nebraska 68970
Tel: 402/746-3285

Acknowledgments

Breslich & Foss would like to thank Bob Boyd and Jack Cooper from The High Desert Museum, Helen and John Erickson, Adair Law from the Oregon Historical Society, Maggie Harris from the Jefferson National Expansion Memorial, Linda Morgese from the Hackley School Library, and Francia White for their assistance.

Picture Credits

The Anschutz Collection Photo: James O. Milmoe: p.38 (top center).

State of California Department of Parks and Recreation: p.35 (center).

California State Library, Sacramento, California: p.5 (top), p. 33 (top left).

Museum of Church History and Art, Salt Lake City: p.15 (bottom left).

The Denver Public Library, Western History Department: p.8 (center left), p.29 (top center).

Helen Erickson: p.11 (top center), p.17 (top right).

Fort Laramie: p.34 (center right).

The High Desert Museum, Bend, Oregon: p.7 (bottom right), p.8 (bottom left), p.10 (bottom right), p.11 (bottom center), p.12 (top left), p.13 (bottom left), p.16 (bottom left), p.17 (bottom center), p.18 (bottom, top right), p.19 (top right), p.20 (center left), p.21 (top right), p.26 (bottom left), p.27 (top right, bottom left), p.29 (bottom center), p.30-31 (center), p.31 (center right, bottom left, bottom center), p.34 (center left), p.35 (bottom right), p.37 (center right, center left), p.40 (top left, bottom right), p.41 (bottom left), p.42 (bottom right), p.42-43 (top center), p.43 (top right, bottom right).

The Huntingdon Library, San Marino, California: p.9 (top left), p.30 (top left), p.32 (left center), p.37 (top center).

James K. Polk Memorial Association, Columbia, Tennessee: p.5 (bottom left).

Jefferson National Expansion Historical Association, St. Louis, Missouri: p. 5 (top right), p.10 (left), p.10-11 (center), p.11 (center right), p.13 (bottom right), p.14 (bottom left), p.14-15 (bottom center), p.15 (top right), p.19 (bottom right), p.22 (bottom center, bottom right), p.23 (bottom right), p.25 (top right, bottom right), p.26 (top left, center left), p.27 (center right), p.28 (center left, bottom right), p.35 (center right, center left), p.39 (center right).

Joslyn Art Museum, Omaha, Nebraska: p.34 (top center).

The Los Angeles Athletic Club Art Collection Photo: Lawrence Reynolds: p.16 (top center).

National Archives: p.32 (top center).

Museum of New Mexico: p.40 (top center).

Collection of the New-York Historical Society: p.39 (top center).

The Oakland Museum History Department: p.18 (top left), p.38 (top left).

Oregon Historical Society, Portland, Oregon: p.6 (center left, center right), p.7 (center), p.8 (bottom center), p.9 (bottom left), p.13 (center right), p.14-15 (center), p.16 (top left), p.20-21 (top center), p.22 (center left), p.24 (top right, bottom left), p.26-27 (bottom center), p.28-29 (center), p.33 (center right), p.36 (center left), p.39 (bottom left), p.41 (top left, bottom right), p.42 (bottom left), p.43 (top left).

Stanford University Museum of Art, Gift of Jane L. Stanford: p.30 (center left).

The Thomas Gilcrease Institute of American History and Art: p.32 (bottom center).

Walters Art Gallery, Baltimore: p.21 (center left).